Ganesh

Subhadra Sen Gupta has written over thirty books for children. Right now she is waiting for a time machine so that she can travel to the past and join Emperor Akbar for lunch. She loves to travel, flirt with cats and chat with autorickshaw drivers. If you want to discuss anything under the sun with her, email her at subhadrasg@gmail.com

Tapas Guha has been working for more than twenty years as an illustrator. He loves to draw comics and illustrate children's books. Ruskin Bond is one of his favourite authors and he loves Tintin comics.

Ganesh

Subhadra Sen Gupta

Illustrated by TAPAS GUHA

RED TURTLE
RUPA

Published in Red Turtle by
Rupa Publications India Pvt. Ltd 2016
7/16, Ansari Road, Daryaganj
New Delhi 110002

Sales centres:
Allahabad Bengaluru Chennai
Hyderabad Jaipur Kathmandu
Kolkata Mumbai

Text copyright © Subhadra Sen Gupta 2004, 2016

Illustration copyright © Tapas Guha 2004, 2016

First published by India Book House Pvt. Ltd, 2004

All rights reserved.
No part of this publication may be reproduced, transmitted,
or stored in a retrieval system, in any form or by any means,
electronic, mechanical, photocopying, recording or otherwise,
without the prior permission of the publisher.

ISBN: 978-81-291-4029-6

First impression 2016

10 9 8 7 6 5 4 3 2 1

The moral right of the author has been asserted.

Printed by Lustra Print Process Pvt. Ltd. New Delhi

This book is sold subject to the condition that it shall not, by way of
trade or otherwise, be lent, resold, hired out, or otherwise circulated,
without the publisher's prior consent, in any form of binding or cover
other than that in which it is published.

Contents

How Ganesh Lost His Head   6

Ganesh Loses a Tusk   23

Ganesh Versus Kartik   30

Ganesh Curses the Moon   37

How Ganesh Lost His Head

You will probably agree with me that there is something funny about Ganesh. All the other Hindu gods, including his father Shiv and his younger brother Kartik, have such handsome faces. But Ganesh has tiny eyes, big floppy ears and a long trunk. The other gods stand tall and proud, like warriors. Ganesh is plump, has a rounded well-fed belly and is definitely not the athletic warrior type. He likes to eat, to read and to dance, and always enjoys a good joke.

How did this happy-go-lucky god end up with an elephant's head? Why not choose the head of a powerful lion or a heroic eagle? What happened to Ganesh to make him so unusual?

It all began when Shiv and his wife, the goddess Parvati, were living on Mount Kailash, high up in the mountain ranges of the Himalayas. Shiv was always busy meditating, sitting cross-legged under a tree with his eyes closed, refusing to talk. If wanderlust hit him he would just pick up his trident and set off on a hiking trip. Poor Parvati was bored. There she was, stuck on a mountaintop with no music, no

dancing, no other goddesses to chat with, and only the forest animals for company. She thought it would be so much nicer if she could play with a child of her own.

So, one morning in her bath, Parvati rubbed fragrant oils on her skin and, with the scurf collected from her body, created a lovely little boy. Holding the child in her arms, she gently blew her sacred breath into his face. The dark eyes opened and he was alive! Parvati was delighted with the boy, and called him Ganesh. He was Parvati and Shiv's eldest child.

A proud Parvati now wanted to show off her handsome son. Shiv agreed it would be a good idea to hold a grand feast. They sent invitations to everyone in Swarg, the Hindu heaven,

to visit them at Mount Kailash and bless the new baby. Swarg lies hidden somewhere in the valleys and mountain peaks of the remotest part of the Himalayas. Here live all the gods, each of their palaces surrounded by large beautiful gardens. Swarg also has celestial dancers, called apsaras, and musicians, called gandharvs, to entertain the deities. Everyone—gods, goddesses, apsaras and gandharvs—was invited to the feast.

When the day arrived, Shiv and Parvati's home became quite crowded. Brahma, who had created the universe, came flying in on his swan, carrying the holy waters of the Ganga

river in a jar. Vishnu, who preserves the universe, flew in on his half-bird, half-human vehicle called Garud. Then, with a roar of thunder and lightning flaring around his head, Indra, the commander of Swarg's army, appeared, riding his giant white elephant named Airavat.

Surya, the sun god, drove a chariot pulled by seven white horses, his golden face dazzling everyone at the gathering. Surya's sister Ushas, the beautiful goddess of dawn, was also there, wearing jewellery as bright as the first rays of the sun. She was followed by Agni, the fire god, and Varun, the god of the sky.

Shiv welcomed them all and led them to a specially decorated hall. It was covered in wild flowers and filled with the perfume of a thousand lotuses. The gandharvs were playing music, the apsaras were dancing and everyone was enjoying the party. Parvati looked around proudly. 'What a wonderful gathering for my son!' she thought, and a happy smile spread across her face.

As she sat with her handsome son in her lap, all the gods and goddesses came up to Parvati to see the child. Brahma

clasped his prayer beads and looked into the bright eyes of the little boy. 'Ah! You have a very intelligent son, dear Parvati,' he pronounced. 'He will be both wise and clever. No one will ever fool him.'

Vishnu smiled and said, 'You are right! And he will also be very brave. He will defeat the biggest and fiercest demons and will always protect his mother.'

One by one, all the guests praised the child and blessed him, making Parvati very happy. But she noticed that there

was one god who, oddly, did not seem interested in her son. Shani, the god of the planet Saturn, was sitting apart in one corner of the hall, his head bent, looking at the floor. He had not come anywhere near the child.

Parvati walked up to Shani and asked politely, 'My lord, have I done something to displease you? You look so unhappy.'

Oh no, not at all, my lady!' Shani shook his head, but still kept his head down and his eyes lowered.

'Then why don't you come to see and bless my son?' Parvati demanded. 'All the gods have praised him, except you. Don't you like children, Lord Shani?'

'Oh, I love children. And I am sure your son is a wonderful child.'

'How would you know? You haven't even looked at him.' Parvati was now quite annoyed. This was a very strange guest. First he came to the feast and then he was rude to his hostess! 'I am insulted, Lord Shani,' she said, her eyes beginning to flash like sparks from a fire.

'But Devi Parvati, you know I have been cursed with the evil eye,' Shani pleaded. 'That is why I never look at anyone's face too closely. If I do, I always harm the person in some way. I don't want to hurt Ganesh.' Shani looked worried.

Parvati smiled confidently. 'I am a goddess and he is my son. I created him. No one can harm him. So I invite you, Shani Devta, lord of the planet Saturn, to come and bless my Ganesh.'

Shani turned to the gathering and said, 'Honoured ones, you have now seen that I am going to look upon Ganesh only because Devi Parvati insists I do so. Please do not blame me if anything goes wrong.'

Everyone nodded at Shani's words. He walked slowly to the cradle where the little boy sat playing.

Then Shani raised his eyes and looked straight at Ganesh's face.

At that very moment, to everyone's horror, Ganesh's head fell off his body and burnt to ashes. The child lay bleeding in his cradle. Parvati screamed. As she ran to snatch up her son, the rest of the gathering seemed paralysed with shock. Then, hearing his wife's sobs, Shiv raised his trident to kill Shani, but Vishnu stood between them.

'It is not Shani's fault, Shiv,' he reminded the shocked father. 'It was Parvati who insisted that Shani look at the child.'

Parvati begged Shiv to find a way to save her son. He asked his two companions, Nandi the bull and Bhringi the demon, to set out immediately. 'Look for a living creature lying with its head towards the north,' he said.

'Should we capture the creature and bring him here?' Nandi asked.

'No,' said Shiv. 'Just cut off its head and bring it to me. Now hurry!'

So Nandi and Bhringi ran out of the hall and began their search. Now, sleeping with the head towards the north used to be thought unlucky, and no human being, god, apsara or gandharv could be found asleep in this position. But Nandi and Bhringi found a white elephant lying with its head pointing towards the north.

Nandi looked at the elephant and said, 'Our master said any living creature, so an elephant's head should do, shouldn't it?'

But Bhringi looked nervous. 'This animal is huge! It could trample us to death if it wakes up!'

They drew their swords and attacked the sleeping elephant.

Disturbed so rudely, the animal struggled to its feet, bellowing in rage. A moment later, Nandi and Bhringi were horrified to see Indra come rushing angrily towards them.

'Stop, you fools! What are you trying to do? Leave my elephant alone!' yelled the furious god.

'Y-your elephant? Is this is your eleph-elephant, s-sir?' stammered Nandi.

'Of course it is. I came to the feast riding my elephant Airavat. Why are you attacking him?'

'He was lying with his head pointing to the north,' explained Bhringi.

'Our master Lord Shiv wants his head,' said Nandi.

'Shiv can't have Airavat's head!' said Indra, springing onto the elephant's back and brandishing his most

powerful weapon, the thunderbolt. 'You will have to fight me first.'

And so began a battle between Indra, and Shiv's army of demons. The sky darkened. Silver-blue streaks of lightning zigzagged across the clouds and struck the demons, turning them to ash. Then it began to pour with rain.

Hearing the commotion, Shiv came to investigate, and discovered a raging battle. He was furious when Nandi explained to him what had happened. 'How dare Indra defy me! I want Airavat's head now.' And he flung his trident through the air where it broke Indra's

thunderbolt in two.

With Shiv himself joining the fray, Indra thought it best to surrender. He bowed before Shiv, the powerful god of destruction, and begged, 'Please, great lord, do not kill my elephant Airavat. He is the best fighting elephant in the world. How can I lead the army of the gods without him?'

Shiv would not listen. He ordered Nandi to chop off Airavat's head, and then he placed it on Ganesh's body. The child immediately came alive.

Parvati could hardly believe what she saw. Her son had the body of a little boy and the head of an elephant! 'What have you done?' she wailed. 'This is not my son!'

No one had the power to change things now. The boy certainly looked odd, but he was alive. Brahma turned to comfort Parvati: 'Devi, be patient and stop weeping. My blessing will make your son the best-loved god. Not even Vishnu or Shiva will have as many devotees as Ganesh. People will adore his kind, smiling elephant head and make sculptures and paintings of him.'

All the gods gave their special blessings to Ganesh.

'Every home will have an image of Ganesh and he will be worshipped every day,' said Vishnu.

Surya added, 'Ganesh will be prayed to before any other god or goddess.'

'In fact, people will pray to him before they start anything at all,' said Agni. 'He will be the god that brings luck and keeps problems at bay.'

'My son will be the happiest of all the gods!' smiled Shiv.

As Parvati finally wiped away her tears, baby Ganesh played contentedly in her lap. The gods and goddesses began to make their way home.

Vishnu was about to mount Garud when he saw Indra kneeling sorrowfully by the side of the beheaded Airavat. He went up to Indra, hoping to cheer him up.

'Parvati has got her son back but I have lost Airavat,' said

Indra sadly. 'He was the best elephant in the world.'

'You have not lost Airavat,' whispered Vishnu. 'Take the elephant to the sacred lotus pool in Vaikunth, my home in Swarg, and bathe Airavat in its holy waters. Airavat will once again be alive.'

Indra did exactly as Vishnu had advised. He was amazed when his beloved Airavat came walking out of the lotus pool with his trunk raised in greeting. Then the elephant trumpeted joyfully as a happy Indra rode him home to his palace.

So both Ganesh and Airavat lost their heads but found them again. That is the magic of Swarg!

Ganesh Loses a Tusk

Ganesh is a bookworm. He not only reads a lot but is also known for inscribing the Mahabharata, that long, long poem describing the great battle fought at Kurukshetra by the Kauravs against their five Pandav cousins.

Now, a close look at Ganesh reveals that he has only one tusk. He lost the other one because of the Mahabharata. In ancient times, all books were written in the form of poetry, which you will agree is not an easy task. Ved Vyas, the sage who composed the verses of the Mahabharata, needed some place quiet and peaceful for his work. So he moved high into the Himalayas and settled down in a cave in the beautiful village of Mana beside the Alakananda river.

Ved Vyas would compose poetry on the banks of the flowing river and then carefully write it down. But on some days he would be so inspired that the rhyme flowed out of his head faster than his hands could write. The lines would then get jumbled up and, at times, Ved Vyas would even forget a whole stanza!

He was pacing up and down the river one morning when Shiv happened to pass by. 'Ah, Ved Vyas!' he called. 'Why the glum face so early in the morning? Are your lines not rhyming?'

Ved Vyas was happy to discuss his problem. 'I need someone who can take down what I say. I must find a scribe who can write really fast.'

'Ask my son Ganesh. He always has his big nose in a book and I'm sure he will enjoy being your scribe.' Ved Vyas thought this an excellent suggestion. He found Ganesh munching on some sweets and playing with his rat.

'Lord, I have a problem...' began the sage.

'Why, what is it?' asked Ganesh. 'Are the Sanskrit spellings giving you a headache? Eat a modak, it'll cheer you up.'

'No thank you, and I have no trouble with spelling! My Sanskrit is perfect, my poetry is beautiful, and the book is coming along well,' responded Ved Vyas quickly. Then he explained his problem. 'Won't you help me, Ganesh? After all, you help everyone.'

Ganesh looked thoughtful. The idea of being forced to work hard at anything at all did not appeal to this lazy god. He

quickly devised a plan to avoid work on Ved Vyas's endless poem.

'I'll help you, but on one condition. You must not make me pause while writing.'

'What do you mean by that?' Ved Vyas was puzzled.

'Once I start, I do not want to stop writing for even a second till the book is finished. If you make me wait while you compose your verses, I won't go on. You must not stop dictating or I will stop writing.'

Ved Vyas nodded. 'Done! I will stop only to take a breath. I will compose and you will write night and day.'

So Ganesh moved in with Ved Vyas. He brought with him a large bundle of dry palm leaves to write on, an enormous bottle of ink and a bunch of sharpened bamboo pens. He sat on a comfortable cushion, chose a pen, dipped it in the ink and

said, 'Start!' Ved Vyas, eyes shut and concentrating hard, recited the lines as he composed them. All the while Ganesh's pen flew across the palm leaves, recording every word.

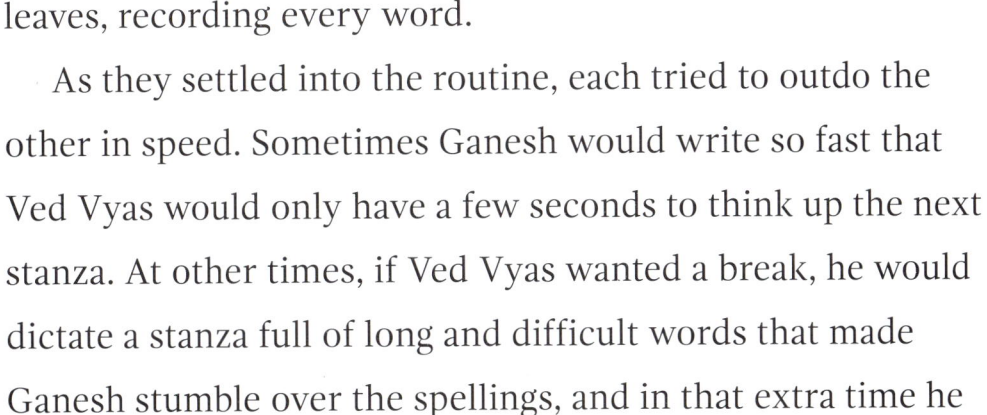

As they settled into the routine, each tried to outdo the other in speed. Sometimes Ganesh would write so fast that Ved Vyas would only have a few seconds to think up the next stanza. At other times, if Ved Vyas wanted a break, he would dictate a stanza full of long and difficult words that made Ganesh stumble over the spellings, and in that extra time he would take a short rest.

One day, Ved Vyas's verse was especially inspired. Ganesh was being made to write faster and faster. First one bamboo pen broke, and then another, and then the third. Ganesh looked around but he had run clean out of pens. Ved Vyas sat before him, smiling triumphantly. Was Ganesh going to lose the race?

'Shall I stop while you sharpen some pens?' asked Ved Vyas.

'No need for that,' said Ganesh, and broke off one of his ivory tusks. Dipping its pointed tip in ink, he calmly continued to write.

And this is how Ganesh completed the Mahabharata, a poem over a hundred thousand stanzas long, the longest poem in the world. Because he now has only one tusk he is called Ekadant, or the One-toothed.

Even today, in Mana near the pilgrim town of Badrinath, they say that the cave called Vyas Gumpha is where the sage

composed his immortal verse. The thin sheets of rock to be seen here are thought to be the pages of the Mahabharata inscribed by Ganesh.

Ganesh Versus Kartik

Kartik was Shiva and Parvati's second son. Unlike Ganesh, Kartik was full of energy and, with his skill in archery and sword fighting, soon became a famous warrior. He had no time for books and seldom ate more than was necessary.

These two brothers never missed an opportunity to compete against the other. Each one tried to be the cleverer, the quicker, the better at studies or at fighting battles. One day, as Kartik painstakingly polished his sword, Ganesh danced around him. 'You don't need brains to wave a sword, Kartik,' he teased, 'just a lot of muscle.'

'Sure,' grinned Kartik. 'I have muscle, but your stomach is

getting so fat that one day you will need to be carried about in a cart.'

Now, Ganesh did not like his little brother laughing at his pot belly. 'I'm not fat! I can move faster than you,' he insisted. Kartik giggled in reply.

Parvati overheard them squabbling. 'Why don't the two of you run a race tomorrow morning to prove who is faster?' she suggested. 'Start from Mount Kailash and go all the way around the earth. The one who returns first will be given a prize.'

Kartik was very excited; he was sure to win. Ganesh looked rather worried.

'So that I can be sure that you do go all the way around,' continued Parvati, 'when you return I will question you about the countries, forests, rivers, oceans and mountains of the world.'

Ganesh had trouble sleeping that night. He knew he was too fat and too unfit. He was about to be defeated by his little brother. Even if he rode on his pet rat he would move too slowly. Energetic Kartik would leap on to his peacock, circle the earth and soon return home. And how was Ganesh to cross the rivers and the oceans? His poor rat would drown!

The next morning Parvati waved her sons off on their race. Within seconds Kartik and his peacock were just a tiny speck in the sky. Ganesh, with a bulging cloth bag slung over his shoulder, rode astride his tiny rat. They went very, very slowly up the hill and Parvati laughed as they disappeared over the top.

Out of sight, Ganesh hopped off his rat. He made himself comfortable in the shade of a tree. Then he eagerly removed a large box of food from his bag and was soon crunching on

potato fries and gulping down soft sweet laddus. He had also packed a bundle of books. Ganesh happily munched and read the day away.

Next morning, to Parvati's utter surprise, Ganesh came down the road with a huge grin on his face!

'I don't believe this! Have you already been around the world?'

'Of course, Amma. Continents, oceans, rivers, mountains…I know them all.'

'On that fat, lazy rat?' Parvati was very suspicious. Ganesh just smiled mysteriously.

Just then Kartik swooped in on his peacock and glared at Ganesh. 'This is impossible! I'm quite sure you did not go all the way round the world.'

'Well then, let me test you both on what you saw,' said Parvati. She asked a lot of questions and both Ganesh and Kartik answered them correctly.

'Ganesh was the first to come home and has answered all the questions, so I declare him the winner,' said Parvati as she

placed a golden crown on her eldest child. Later, when she was alone with Ganesh, she said, 'I don't believe you went around the world.'

'Well, Amma, my body didn't, but my mind travelled far and wide. I spent the night under a tree just over the hill.'

'But then, how did you know the answers?'

'I read them in my books!' Ganesh grinned. 'That's what I had in my bag—a good encyclopaedia and an atlas and, of course, something to eat. Kartik never reads books and so he knows very little. I discover the world in books.'

'Ah, my clever son!' laughed Parvati as she hugged Ganesh. 'You cheated in the race but I give you full marks for using your brain!'

Ganesh Curses the Moon

All year Ganesh looks forward to his birthday. On this day, known as Ganesh Chaturthi, which falls either in August or September, everyone presents the god with his favourite things—sweets and candies, sugared drinks and dreamy creamy desserts.

One birthday, many ages ago, Ganesh outdid himself. He tucked into trays piled with laddus, modaks, barfis, gulab jamuns and rasgullas, and tall glasses of lassi and sherbet. He ate and ate and smiled and smiled, blessing everyone with good fortune and happiness.

After the birthday party was over, an exhausted Ganesh struggled down from his throne and sighed. He could hardly walk! He sent for his rat and clambered onto his back. 'Take me home, my friend,' he said.

Ganesh was a hefty load on any day, but on this night he was even heavier! The poor rat huffed and puffed along while Ganesh stretched and yawned and tried to make him move faster.

Suddenly, a snake slithered across their path. The rat sprang up in fright and leapt behind a bush.

Ganesh was sent tumbling to the ground. As he landed with a thud, his stomach burst open. All the sweets that he had eaten toppled out. Absolutely furious, Ganesh grabbed the snake and, using it as a belt, fastened his belly together again. The rat, meanwhile, had vanished. He had no intention of being eaten by a snake!

'Stupid rat!' Ganesh muttered. 'Now I'll have to walk home. Why is he so afraid of a snake? After all, I am a god. I'll protect him.'

Just then he heard a chuckle. He looked around in surprise but there was no one to be seen. Fuming and fretting, Ganesh waddled on.

'I really should not eat so much. I am getting much too fat,' he thought. Again there was laughter, and this time there seemed to be a great many people enjoying the joke.

Ganesh looked up. Chandra, the moon god, was roaring with laughter, the stars were giggling, and the entire sky was swaying with mirth. And

they were laughing at poor Ganesh!

He was furious. How dare they laugh at him, and on his birthday too! Ganesh shouted up at the moon, 'I curse you, Chandra! You will lose all your light and become dark and useless!'

At once the sky turned pitch black. The moon seemed to have been switched off. The stars began to cry and the forest animals started bumping into each other and tripping over rocks and slipping into puddles.

'What have you done?' Chandra demanded. 'It is my job to light up the night. The world can do nothing in the dark.'

'Well then, you should not have laughed at me,' said Ganesh, stumbling along.

Chandra changed his tone. 'Forgive me, my lord,' he begged. 'You are the kindest and most lovable of the gods. Please remove your curse on me.'

Now, unlike Shiv who can be quite vengeful, his gentle son was already feeling sorry that he had lost his temper. Besides, he knew it would be very difficult to move around without moonlight.

'All right, all right,' he said. 'But from now on, Chandra, you will no longer shine brightly every night. Your light will increase gradually for a fortnight until purnima night, when you will shine round and full.

'Then, for the next fourteen days, you will get dimmer and dimmer until you turn completely dark on amavasya night. That is when you will be sorry for your rudeness today.'

So now you know why the moon waxes and wanes in the sky—it is because Chandra once laughed at overfed, roly-poly Ganesh.